D1555613

FASCINATING FACTS ABOUT LAS VEGAS

FASCINATING
FACTS ABOUT
LAS VEGAS

VICTOR DORFF

FALL RIVER PRESS

New York

FALL RIVER PRESS

New York

An Imprint of Sterling Publishing
387 Park Avenue South
New York, NY 10016

Design by Gavin Motnyk

ISBN 978-1-4351-4192-6 (print format)

Distributed in Canada by Sterling Publishing
c/o Canadian Manda Group, 165 Dufferin Street
Toronto, Ontario, Canada M6K 3H6
Distributed in the United Kingdom by GMC Distribution Services
Castle Place, 166 High Street, Lewes, East Sussex, England BN7
1XU
Distributed in Australia by Capricorn Link (Australia) Pty. Ltd.
P.O. Box 704, Windsor, NSW 2756, Australia

For information about custom editions, special sales, and premium and corporate purchases, please contact Sterling Special Sales
at 800-805-5489 or specialsales@sterlingpublishing.com.

Manufactured in United States of America

2   4   6   8   10   9   7   5   3   1

www.sterlingpublishing.com

To my parents, Norman and Dorothy, who were married in Las Vegas. Thanks for imbuing life with the spirit of showmanship, glamour, luxury, taking a chance . . . and lots of laughs.

INTRODUCTION

If you have a fantasy, it can be fulfilled in Las Vegas.

Whatever it is, there is someone waiting there to make it happen for you.

The city seems to know what you want even before you do, and makes it readily available, for a price—from world-class art and ultra-luxe recreation, to cheap (and not-so-cheap) thrills and adrenaline-pumping adventure.

Enduring both the scorn and secret admiration of outsiders for more than 100 years, Las Vegas has found ways to keep people coming back for more.

Surviving one boom-bust cycle after another with creativity and guts, the city entered the 21st century as a fantasy playground unlike any other.

Today, children of all ages come to Las Vegas for jaw-dropping, eye-popping entertainment—no holds barred, no judgments made.

What the city has come to embody is a secret society open to everyone, with the promise, "What happens in Vegas, stays in Vegas."

Maybe it does; maybe it doesn't.

In the end, that's not what matters.

What counts are the memories—the ones that are real, and the ones you make up on the way home.

So, relax and enjoy!

More than 11,000 years ago,

the region now called the Las Vegas Valley offered water and vegetation to nomadic tribes wandering through a brutal desert.

One after another, Native American civilizations made homes by the Las Vegas oasis, never knowing they were living in what would become the entertainment capital of the world.

Even when Europeans "discovered" the area in the 1820s, they only saw a stopover location on the long and dusty road to California.

Now, we know better.

Las Vegas has playfully

accepted many monikers in its relatively brief history as a city.

- Sin City
- City of Lights
- The City That Never Sleeps
- The Entertainment Capital of the World
- The Wedding Capital

Other cities may also claim those titles. Las Vegas doesn't seem to care.

Jedediah Smith

is credited with being the first American explorer to enter the Las Vegas Valley in 1827 in his quest for new fur-trapping regions.

Rafael Rivera was a scout with a trading party blazing the Old Spanish Trail from New Mexico to California in 1829, when he broke north in search of water and found Las Vegas Springs.

Ultimately, however, it was John C. Fremont who put the area on the map, literally, in 1844. He reported finding gushing springs that made for "a delightful bathing place" and turned Las Vegas into a mecca for many weary travelers.

First came the Mormons.

In June 1855, 30 missionaries arrived to build a 150-square-foot adobe fort, the first permanent structure in the region. They farmed the land and mined the nearby mountains, creating an outpost along the path from Utah to California.

After less than two years, difficulties with the local natives and internal disputes brought the experiment to an end, and they headed back to Utah.

The site of the Old Las Vegas Mormon Fort is now a Nevada state park in downtown Las Vegas, and part of the original structure is still visible.

Octavius D. Gass

knew an opportunity when he saw it.

In 1865, the miner built a large ranch on the site of the Old Las Vegas Mormon Fort, providing a way station—with a store and a blacksmith shop—for travelers through the desert.

To keep the ranch running, Gass periodically borrowed money, using the land as collateral.

In 1881, after borrowing $5,000 in gold, Gass defaulted and lost the Las Vegas Ranch.

Archibald and Helen Stewart

took the Las Vegas Ranch from O.D. Gass, foreclosing on his loan in 1881.

A few years later, after Archibald was killed in a gun battle, Helen decided to stay on the ranch with her five children.

She ran the property successfully, acquiring more land and water rights until the Stewart Ranch covered 1,800 acres of the Las Vegas Valley.

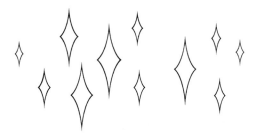

In the early 20th century,

gold and silver were discovered in the region around Las Vegas, creating a nascent mining industry and a population boom.

Senator William A. Clark of Montana saw the potential profit in building a railroad to link California and Utah.

The location and water supply of Las Vegas made it an obvious place for the trains to stop, just as it had been for travelers on foot, so Clark sent surveyors to scout for a station.

The spot the Mormons

had picked for their fort in 1855 was the right place for a railroad station nearly 50 years later.

Helen Stewart sold most of her ranch and water rights to the railroad in 1902 for $55,000.

She and her children continued to live on the remaining land until her death in 1926.

J.T. McWilliams,

a surveyor who knew the railroad was coming, turned the birth of Las Vegas into its own tale of two cities.

In 1904, McWilliams bought 80 acres of land west of the Stewart ranch and laid out what he called the "Original Las Vegas Town site."

Advertising in Los Angeles newspapers, he sold the lots for $200 each, but a lack of supplies and water, combined with the searing desert heat, made for very unpleasant living conditions.

The railroad

sold its lots on the former Stewart Ranch at an auction on May 15, 1905.

People came from far and wide to bid for their piece of the future.

Almost immediately after the railroad sold off its parcels of land, with their abundant water supply, McWilliams's "Original Las Vegas Town site" was all but abandoned.

LAS VEGAS WEATHER FACTS

The sun shines

more than 300 days a year.

The average daily extreme temperatures range from a low of 34 degrees and a high of 58 degrees (in December and January) to a low of 74 degrees and a high of 106 degrees (in July).

The record extremes were 8 degrees (January 13, 1963) and 117 degrees (July 24, 1942 *and* July 19, 2005).

The average annual precipitation is 4.25 inches, with the extremes being 2.6 inches of rain on August 20–21, 1957, and 9 inches of snow on January 3–4, 1974.

During the first

land auction in 1905, the railroad designated
Blocks 16 and 17 as two zones where liquor
could be sold without restriction.

Block 16, bordered by Stewart, Ogden,
First, and Second streets, became the red-
light district, where prostitution thrived.

Alcohol was readily available on Block
16 (even during Prohibition), and the city
turned a blind eye toward the sex trade.

Just prior to World War II,

the U.S. Army threatened to forbid personnel from entering Las Vegas if the brothels of Block 16 weren't closed. In January 1942, the liquor and slot machine licenses for all the establishments on Block 16 were cancelled.

Today, all of Block 16 is a parking lot.

Fremont Street

is the epicenter of the growth of Las Vegas—the heart of downtown.

The initial property auction that launched the city took place at the intersection of Fremont and Main.

Fremont was the first street in Las Vegas to be paved (in 1925) and the site of the first traffic light in town.

In 1956, the Fremont Hotel and Casino became the city's first high-rise hotel, and it is still in operation today.

The Hotel Nevada

opened in 1906 on a plot of land that cost $1,750 the year before.

Patrons got a "first class," 100-square-foot room with electric lights for $1 a day.

When the Stardust opened in 1958, its rooms cost $6 a day.

The average nightly Las Vegas hotel room rate in 2011 was $105.

The first hotel

in Las Vegas opened the same day—May 15, 1905—the railroad began auctioning off lots in the new development.

The Las Vegas Hotel was nothing more than a tent built on a 140-foot wooden structure.

It had 30 beds, a dining room, and a bar.

The first phone

in Las Vegas was installed in the Hotel Nevada in 1907.

(The hotel's phone number was, literally, 1.)

In 1931, when gambling was once-again legal, the hotel changed its name to Sal Sagev (Las Vegas, backwards).

In 1955, the Golden Gate Casino opened in the hotel, which adopted the same name.

Today, the Golden Gate Hotel and Casino is the oldest hotel in Las Vegas.

The Golden Gate

Hotel and Casino introduced generous shrimp cocktails (no lettuce; just shrimp) to its gamblers at a cost of 50 cents in 1959.

The 25-millionth shrimp cocktail was served in 1991, for 99 cents.

The milestone was celebrated with the presence of all four of the mayors who served in office during the intervening 32 years.

Today, the shrimp cocktail is still a Golden Gate specialty, but the price is $1.99.

John C. Fremont

could not have envisioned the street or the "Experience" that bears his name today.

Free concerts and entertainment draw more than 17 million visitors a year to the Fremont Street Experience, an open-air pedestrian mall covering five city blocks in downtown Las Vegas.

The world's largest video screen, the Viva Vision, serves as an overhead canopy, measuring 1,500 feet by 90 feet and hanging 90 feet above the ground.

A 550,000-watt audio system rounds out the multimedia extravaganza in the heart of Downtown Las Vegas.

Zip Lines

are more common in rain forest canopies than city streets, but uncommon is the norm in Las Vegas.

So it shouldn't be a surprise to find that the Fremont Street Experience includes an opportunity to fly through the air at 30 mph, attached to a cable and twirling in the breeze along an 800-foot course.

The ride is available during daylight, but the nighttime run includes the light show from the Viva Vision screen overhead.

As of 2011,

nearly 39 million people visit Las Vegas annually, filling 84 percent of the available hotel rooms (compared to a 60 percent occupancy rate nationwide).

Gambling on the Las Vegas Strip brought in more than $6 billion in revenue during 2011, with the downtown venues generating another half-billion dollars.

Taxes on gaming revenue account for nearly half of the revenue raised by the state of Nevada, which is one reason Nevada residents don't have to pay an income tax.

The Las Vegas

Convention and Visitors Authority says the average visitor spends four nights in Las Vegas, is 49 years old, college-educated, and has a gambling budget of $450.

Was it worth it? More than 90 percent of visitors surveyed reported being "very satisfied" with their visit; fewer than 1 percent were "dissatisfied."

Even visitors

not turned on by sex, booze, gambling, or glitzy entertainment can still find what they are looking for in Las Vegas ... if what they are looking for involves squeezing off a round of ammunition from an Uzi submachine gun, or any number of other steaming hot weapons.

Machine Guns Vegas (MGV) combines a VIP Lounge atmosphere with a wide array of unconventional weapons, including a grenade launcher, for an adrenaline-charged experience.

And, unlike those nasty casinos, kids are welcome at MGV!

Many tourists

who visit Las Vegas have never really been to Las Vegas.

Most of the resort casinos were built on "the Strip," a stretch of road that mostly lies outside the city limits.

Except for the Stratosphere, the Strip hotels are actually in an unincorporated area governed by Clark County.

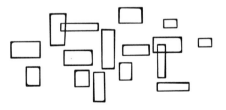

Most towns

have a "Welcome to..." sign, but not very many of those signs make it onto the National Register of Historic Places.

"Welcome to Fabulous Las Vegas" did.

Designed in 1959 by Betty Willis for the city, the sign cost $4,000 to build and has stood on the median at the south end of the Strip ever since.

In 2008,

after decades of tolerating furtive photographers illegally parking and jaywalking to get a shot of the iconic "Welcome to Fabulous Las Vegas" sign, county officials installed a 12-space parking lot and walkway adjacent to the site.

The lot, which cost $400,000, also includes a parking lane for tour buses and limousines.

Betty Willis

never trademarked the design of her "Welcome to Fabulous Las Vegas" sign, so copies have appeared in other parts of town, and the image has shown up on countless souvenirs.

Willis says she intended the sign to be a gift to the city, so she doesn't mind that it is in the public domain.

Bulbs that have illuminated

the "Welcome to Fabulous Las Vegas" sign are available for sale at OfficialLasVegas-Light.com.

Lights for Locals, the organization behind this novel souvenir idea, uses the revenues to support local charities.

Bulbs come in a display box with a certificate of authenticity that even identifies the position the bulb had on the sign and the date the bulb was removed.

A premium is charged for bulbs signed by celebrities who perform in Las Vegas.

Thomas Young

sold his first neon sign to the Oasis Café in Las Vegas in 1932, establishing a foothold for his sign company that is still secure in the city today.

The Age of Neon began in Las Vegas in 1945, when YESCO (the Young Electric Sign Company) installed the first glowing casino-hotel sign for the Boulder Club.

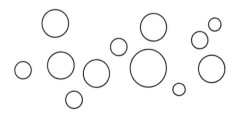

Vegas Vic,

the 40-foot-tall neon cowboy that welcomed visitors to the Pioneer Club on Fremont Street, was the largest mechanical sign in the world when it was built by YESCO in 1951.

The cowboy, who was originally a cartoon figure created for the Chamber of Commerce, waved his arm, winked, blew smoke from his cigarette, and called out, "Howdy, Podner" every 15 minutes.

In the 1980s

a giant neon cowgirl was added to the scenery, above a strip joint called Sassy Sally.

She's known as Vegas Vicky now, having married Vegas Vic in a ceremony covered by the local media when both signs were temporarily removed to make way for the Fremont Street Experience.

Both Vegas Vic and Vegas Vicky

are back in full view these days.

Vic can still be seen (but not heard) welcoming visitors to the souvenir shop that now occupies the former Pioneer Club.

Vicky presides over the Girls of Glitter Gulch, downtown's only strip club.

In the late 1950s,

YESCO (formerly the Young Electric Sign Company) was responsible for the historic neon displays at the Mint, the Silver Slipper, the Stardust, and the Golden Nugget casinos.

In later years, Circus Circus, the Sahara, Caesars Palace... even McCarran International Airport turned to YESCO to design and install their signs.

Today, YESCO's work is still a big part of the Las Vegas landscape, including efforts to restore the classic signs and return them to full operation.

The Neon Museum

was established in 1996 to protect and to preserve the art form that is practically synonymous with Las Vegas.

More than 150 signs have been collected, and many more have been promised to the museum when the time comes to turn out their lights.

The Neon Museum and the YESCO Boneyard, where old signs sit and await resurrection, are open for tours by appointment only.

The Neon Museum

uses the entire city as its display case.

The first historic sign restored was the Hacienda Horse and Rider, which originally adorned the Hacienda Hotel in 1967. Today, the sign is located at the intersection of Fremont Street Experience and Las Vegas Boulevard.

Aladdin's Lamp from the Aladdin Hotel (1966) and The Flame from the roof of the Flame Restaurant (1961) are at the same intersection.

The Chief Court Hotel sign (1940) and Andy Anderson, the Anderson Dairy mascot (1956) are both at the intersection of Fremont Street Experience and Fourth Street.

The U.S. Department of Transportation

has named the Las Vegas Strip one of America's "National Scenic Byways."

Only 3.4 miles long, the stretch of Las Vegas Boulevard between Sahara and Washington avenues was added to the list in 2009.

In recommending the drive, which takes about 15 minutes, the Byways Program specifically mentions the neon signs that adorn the roadway, saying they "possess the charm and aesthetic appeal that make this section of Las Vegas Boulevard a must-see."

Benny Binion's Horseshoe,

originally installed outside the Horse-
shoe Hotel and Casino in 1951, is one of
three vintage neon signs erected along the
stretch of Las Vegas Boulevard now designated a National Scenic Byway.

The Silver Slipper and the Bow & Arrow
Motel sign, both from the 1950s, are also
now part of the roadside scenery.

Steve Wynn

was not content to build an impressive video display as the sign in front of his Wynn Las Vegas Hotel. He wanted a "moving eraser" that seemed to change the graphics as it moved across the screen.

The result is a 135-foot-tall sign with a 62,000-pound block that moves up and down across the LED videos. The "eraser" runs on urethane wheels along a steel track, traveling 100 feet in 10 seconds.

Synchronized videos give the appearance of being affected by the movement of the eraser.

For those who fear

a world without sexually explicit material, the Erotic Heritage Museum has stepped in to protect the genre while promoting "Sexuality Education Through the Arts."

Calling itself "the only Sex Museum in Las Vegas," the nonprofit organization is the brainchild of Methodist minister Reverend Ted McIlvenna and pornographer Harry Mohney, who founded the strip club next door.

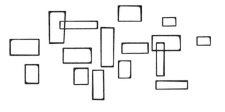

The grand opening

of the Erotic Heritage Museum in 2008 included a wedding performed by an Elvis impersonator. The bride and groom were the same person, who dressed his right side as a man and his left side as a woman for the nuptials.

The museum went on to be named "Best Pick for Culture in Las Vegas" by *944 Magazine* and "Best Museum" by the *Las Vegas Review Journal*.

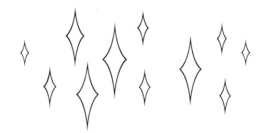

Dr. Laura Henkel,

who helped create the Erotic Heritage Museum as part of her doctoral thesis and was its executive director, later launched the Sin City Gallery as another venue for sexually themed art.

The gallery produces 12 Inches of Sin, the first International Annual Juried Erotic Art Show in Las Vegas.

Sin City Gallery was named the best gallery in Nevada for 2012 by the American Art Awards.

The first woman

to own a funeral parlor in Las Vegas also provided the foundation for the collection of the Clark County Museum.

Anna Roberts Parks, who opened the Palm Mortuary in the 1920s, collected historical and Native American artifacts. After her death, they were given to what was then called the Southern Nevada Museum.

Since then, the museum has expanded to 30 acres and includes the 1931 Union Pacific Depot from Boulder City and the 1966 Candlelight Wedding Chapel (which holds the record for the largest number of weddings in a single day).

Clark County,

home of Las Vegas, issued nearly 90,000 marriage licenses in 2011.

To give that number a context, the County Clerk's office points out that Clark County is home to fewer than 2 million residents.

Now, consider Cook County, Illinois, where Chicago is located: It has more than 5 million residents, but issued fewer than 31,000 marriage licenses.

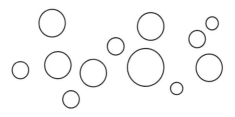

A marriage license

costs $60 cash in Las Vegas.

It costs $5 more to pay with a credit card.

Once the license is issued, there is no waiting period.

Couples who have planned ahead sufficiently to bring a witness and make an appointment can proceed immediately from the license bureau to the Office of Civil Marriages, about a block and a half away.

A wedding there costs $50 cash.

It costs $5 more to pay with a credit card.

Debit cards are not accepted in either office.

Nevada is known

for its offbeat and unconventional weddings, but be advised: *There are limits to what is permitted, even in Las Vegas!*

Marriage licenses will not be issued to couples that are already married, even if they want to renew their vows.

That kind of behavior is *not* legally sanctioned by the state.

The Wee Kirk o' the Heather

is the oldest of the Las Vegas wedding chapels, having opened in 1940.

The chapel has been featured in numerous films over the years, including *Fools Rush In* and *Intolerable Cruelty.*

Okay, maybe those aren't the best references.

But the Wee Kirk offers a wide range of alternatives for the couple looking to get hitched, from the basic chapel package to helicopter weddings in which the vows are exchanged while hovering over one of the many scenic locations in Las Vegas.

Naturally, "Elvis" is always available to perform the ceremony.

Many couples

opt to wed in the Valley of Fire. Dedicated in 1935, it's Nevada's oldest and largest state park.

Other tourists make the 55-mile trek from Las Vegas just for the natural beauty and the 3,000-year-old petroglyphs.

Movie buffs may recognize some of the quintessential desert scenery as the site of Captain James T. Kirk's cinematic death scene in *Star Trek: Generations*, or as Mars in the Arnold Schwarzenegger film, *Total Recall*.

The Little Church of the West

opened in 1942 as part of the Last Frontier Hotel. The structure, which is the oldest on the Las Vegas Strip, is on the National Register of Historic Places, and many celebrities have tied the knot there, including Betty Grable, Judy Garland, Mickey Rooney, Dudley Moore, and—in the world of cinematic fiction—Elvis Presley, when he "married" Ann-Margret in *Viva Las Vegas*.

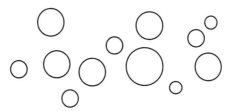

The Little Church of the West

didn't get to be so old by just sitting on its foundation.

In fact, the chapel had to be moved three times to stay clear of the wrecking ball.

It moved to its current location at Russell Road and Las Vegas Boulevard in 1996.

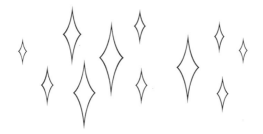

The 70-year-old

Little Church of the West is constructed of cedar and redwood, and the building is not substantially changed from when it was first built.

Therefore, if lighting a candle is an important element of the ceremony a couple has planned, they need to find another place to get married.

Open flames are not allowed in this chapel.

The Little White Wedding Chapel

has been the venue of choice for nearly a million couples since it opened in 1951.

Mickey Rooney was married there. Twice.

(In addition to the time he was married at the Little Church of the West.)

And that was before the Little White Wedding Chapel had a drive-through window.

The Tunnel of Love

at the Little White Wedding Chapel is a 24-hour drive-through marriage service.

It was first conceived in 1991 as a building modification to make weddings more accessible to the handicapped, who might have trouble getting out of their cars.

The idea took off, and the drive-through window is now under a canopy painted with cherubs to help create the appropriate mood for nuptials.

The "World Famous"

Chapel of the Bells, open since 1957, also lays claim to having performed a wedding ceremony in which Mickey Rooney was the groom.

In addition to its celebrity list and an online video testimonial from Kelly Ripa, the chapel website lists the feature films in which it appeared. They include *Honeymoon in Vegas, Indecent Proposal, Mars Attacks,* and *Vegas Vacation.*

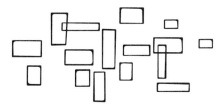

Lots of people get married

in Las Vegas... too many to list them all.

In fact, too many *celebrities* have been married in Las Vegas to name them all.

What follows is a completely unrepresentative list of some of those couples, many of whom (though not all) stayed married for longer than three days.

- Andre Agassi and Steffi Graf
- Angelina Jolie and Billy Bob Thornton
- Betty White and Allen Ludden
- Betty Grable and Harry James
- Britney Spears and Jason Allen Alexander
- Coolio and Josefa Salinas

Fascinating Facts About Las Vegas

- David Cassidy and Kay Lenz
- Dennis Rodman and Carmen Electra
- Elvis Presley and Priscilla
  Ann Beaulieu
- Frank Sinatra and Mia Farrow
- Jane Fonda and Roger Vadim
- Jon Bon Jovi and Dorothea Hurley
- Judy Garland and Mark Herron
- Mary Tyler Moore and Grant Tinker
- Michael Jordan and Juanita Vanoy
- Mike Tyson and Lakiha Spicer
- Paul Newman and Joanne Woodward
- Richard Gere and Cindy Crawford
- Steve Lawrence and Eydie Gorme
- Wayne Newton and Elaine Okamura
- Xavier Cugat and Charo

In Las Vegas,

celebrity weddings are not limited to the famous.

Anyone can put on a white dress and walk down the aisle next to George Clooney... or a life-size facsimile thereof.

That's just one of the attractions at Madame Tussaud's Wax Museum on the Strip.

For the commitment-phobic, the museum has an *American Idol* set, where visitors can have their pictures taken performing before a skeptical Simon Cowell. (Is there any other kind?)

Despite its initial misgivings,

the International Astronomical Union allowed scientists at the Jet Propulsion Laboratory in Pasadena to name a newly discovered asteroid after the city of Las Vegas.

It wasn't questions of moral character that disturbed the International Union. It was all that light pollution!

In the original application, Las Vegas was described as "a valley so bright with laser beams and neon tracery as to be visible from outer space."

Astronomers *hate* that sort of thing.

But, on the occasion of the city's 100th birthday, the scientists relented, and *82332 Las Vegas 2001 LV6* got its name.

Of all the homages

to the human body that can be found in Las Vegas, only one provides a life-size view from the inside out.

Bodies... The Exhibition—the title says it all.

In addition to 13 whole-body human specimens, 260 organs and partial-bodies are on display at the Luxor in various states of dissection.

Arranged by function—muscles, nerves, circulation, respiration... even fetal development—the exhibit provides views of the human body once reserved for medical students and coroners.

The only drive-through

smoke shop in Las Vegas belongs to the Paiute Indian tribe.

At the end of 1911, Helen Stewart deeded 10 acres of downtown Las Vegas to the Paiutes, who had roamed freely throughout the region before the arrival of the railroad.

Today, the tribe is legally a sovereign nation.

It also owns and operates three golf courses in the area.

Gambling

has not *always* been legal in Las Vegas.

In 1910, after much foot-dragging, the Nevada Legislature passed a very strict anti-gambling law to bring the state into compliance with national law.

The rules were so tight, it was illegal even to flip a coin to see who should buy the next round.

It is a safe bet, however, that the law was not strictly obeyed.

The beginning of 1931

marked a turning point for Las Vegas because of three seemingly unrelated events: the legalization of gambling, the relaxation of residency requirements for divorce, and the start of construction on Boulder Dam.

All three of these were part of what would now be referred to as a "stimulus package," and they combined to create a steady stream of revenue in southern Nevada throughout the Depression.

Before the start of construction

on Boulder Dam (which later became known as Hoover Dam), only 5,200 people lived in Las Vegas, then a tiny Western frontier town.

In 1931, when building began, the population increased by nearly 50 percent, as the city's infrastructure expanded to prepare for the coming boom.

The dam site generated a tremendous tourist industry that benefited Las Vegas, too, bringing hundreds of thousands of people into town each year during construction.

The Meadows Club

was one of the first casinos to open after gambling was re-legalized in 1931.

Tony Cornero, a gambler and rum-runner from California, ran the operation, although his brother applied for the gaming license because of Tony's criminal record.

The property was on the road that led to the Boulder Dam site, so it would catch traffic coming into town from that direction, but its nightclub was also popular with the locals.

Frances Gumm

and her sisters were among the acts that played the Meadows Club in the early 1930s.

Gumm later became more popularly known as Judy Garland.

While playing at the Flamingo in 1957, Judy Garland surprised the audience by calling her 11-year-old daughter to the stage to sing a duet.

That was the start of Liza Minnelli's career.

Tony Cornero and his brother

built a hotel in 1931 alongside the Meadows Club, promising to turn the casino into a full-blown resort.

Apparently, they believed that city officials were going to shut down Block 16, the red-light district of Las Vegas, which would have given them a monopoly on prostitution just outside the city limits.

That didn't happen.

The Meadows Club

was the first full-featured combination of a casino, hotel, and restaurant, and it was the first such complex positioned specifically to pick up business from automobile traffic.

As construction of Boulder Dam was winding down in 1935, Tony Cornero and his brother sold the Meadows Club.

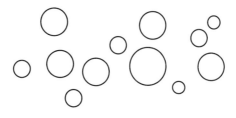

In 1944, Tony Cornero

decided to try owning a casino again.

He and a group of partners opened the SS Rex casino in the Apache Hotel in downtown Las Vegas.

In addition to the regular fare, the SS Rex offered the opportunity to bet on horse races at two tracks in Mexico and one in Cuba.

Cornero had to abandon the SS Rex in 1946 after a dispute with his partners.

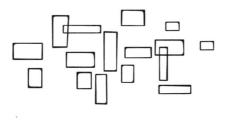

Not one to give up,

Tony Cornero returned to Las Vegas in 1954 with a plan to build the largest resort in the world.

He bought 36 acres on the Strip and began plans for a 1,000-room hotel-casino.

He was able to raise $6 million for the project, even though his criminal past would keep him from ever being able to get a license to run the operation.

The project was nearly three-quarters finished when Cornero died playing craps at the Desert Inn in 1955.

Tony Cornero's dream

was completed in 1958, when the Stardust opened.

The hotel had more than a thousand rooms and both the largest swimming pool and the largest casino in Nevada.

The Stardust continued in operation for nearly three decades and was imploded in 2007 to make way for Echelon Place, a mixed-use development.

The El Cortez Hotel and Casino

was the first major resort in downtown Las Vegas.

Built in 1941 at Sixth and Fremont, the hotel was thought to be too far away from the action to attract enough gamblers to make a profit.

Today, the El Cortez is the oldest continuously operating casino-hotel property in Las Vegas, and it sports the same neon sign that's been atop the building since the 1940s.

In 1945,

mobster Benjamin "Bugsy" Siegel bought the El Cortez for $600,000, a hefty premium over the $245,000 it had cost to build in 1941.

He planned to expand the hotel, but he had trouble getting the city to provide him with the water and electricity he needed.

Six months later, he sold the property, making a $160,000 profit, and he turned his eyes toward the stretch of highway south of town that would later be known as the Las Vegas Strip.

The Hotel El Rancho Vegas

was the first full-scale casino-resort on what would come to be known as the Vegas Strip.

El Rancho's appearance in 1941 created an entirely new breed of vacation destination. Miles from downtown Las Vegas, El Rancho provided everything a guest would need—restaurants, lodging, gambling, stores...

In short, it created the mold from which Las Vegas resorts are still emerging today.

The history of Las Vegas casinos

is one of boom and bust, and whenever money was tight, the Mob was there to offer "help."

After World War II, Billy Wilkerson, owner of the *Hollywood Reporter*, wanted to build a resort on the Strip.

Building materials were in short supply, and in 1946, he ran out of funds.

That was when Bugsy Siegel and his New York "partners" came up with a million dollars to invest.

Siegel named the resort after his redheaded girlfriend with the long legs— the Flamingo.

During construction of the Flamingo,

Bugsy Siegel watched costs soar beyond original estimates, so he decided to raise cash by opening the casino before the hotel was finished.

It was a bad idea.

On December 26, 1946, bad weather delayed many of the guests coming from Los Angeles for the grand opening.

Of those who made it, the gamblers who won took their money to other resorts to spend on rooms and meals.

In its first week of operation, the Flamingo lost $300,000.

It closed after the second week.

The Flamingo's second incarnation

began on March 1, 1947, under a new name: the Fabulous Flamingo.

By April, Bugsy Siegel had forced Billy Wilkerson to sever his ties with the hotel.

Siegel's New York "partners" were growing suspicious of him and feared for the return of their investment.

On June 20, 1947, while spending time at his girlfriend's house in Beverly Hills, Bugsy Siegel was "whacked" by an unknown assassin.

The present-day

Flamingo Hotel contains a bronze plaque honoring Benjamin "Bugsy" Siegel and what it calls the "Bugsy Building."

Siegel had incorporated extensive defense measures into his hotel residence suite. There were bulletproof windows, five escape exits, and dead-end hallways to confuse intruders.

With 20/20 hindsight, the authors of the text on the sign ironically refer to these precautions as "geographically misplaced," considering that Siegel was murdered in California and not in his presumably secure hotel suite.

So, now that he's dead,

where does Bugsy Siegel hang out?

In Las Vegas, of course.

In fact, there are quite a number of ghostly spirits said to make Las Vegas their home, and Haunted Vegas Tours is more than happy to show tourists the most likely spots to glimpse them.

Are Elvis and Liberace dead?

Maybe, but that doesn't mean they don't still draw a crowd.

Moe Sedway,

Morris Rosen, and Gus Greenbaum took over the operation of the Fabulous Flamingo the day after Bugsy Siegel was assassinated.

The resort became a magnet for Hollywood headliners, whose presence helped to turn Las Vegas into a destination for anyone seeking world-class entertainment.

In no time, the Fabulous Flamingo began turning a handsome profit.

When the Moulin Rouge

opened in 1955, it was the first fully integrated resort in Las Vegas.

Up until that point, although black entertainers were allowed to *perform* on the Strip, they were not allowed to gamble, eat, or rent rooms there.

The Moulin Rouge was on the west side of Las Vegas, far from the Strip itself.

By the end of the year, it was closed and in bankruptcy.

During its brief life

as an active casino, the Moulin Rouge had quite an impact.

Blacks and whites made up the standing-room-only crowd that came on opening night to see the all-black stage show.

Dinah Washington, Lionel Hampton, Sammy Davis, Jr., and Frank Sinatra were among the acts that headlined there.

Other stars came to enjoy themselves after performing on the Strip, and they would spontaneously perform for the audiences at the Moulin Rouge as well.

But after it closed, the segregation policy of the Strip remained unchanged... until 1960.

As late as the spring of 1960, segregation rules kept even Sammy Davis, Jr., a member of the famed Rat Pack, from enjoying the amenities of the clubs where he worked.

On March 25, a civil rights demonstration and march down the Strip was scheduled.

A summit meeting with leaders of the NAACP, law enforcement, and the casino owners was hastily arranged and held in the closed Moulin Rouge.

An informal agreement was reached, the color barrier was lifted, blacks were allowed to patronize the Strip, and the march was cancelled.

The Moulin Rouge

hotel rooms were turned into apartments in 1985, but the condition of the property continued to deteriorate.

In 1992, as plans for the revival of the building were brewing, the Moulin Rouge was added to the National Register of Historic Places.

By 1997, however, even the apartments were shut down.

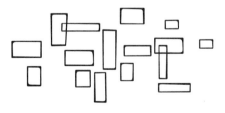

An arson fire

ravaged the Moulin Rouge in 2003 and the building never recovered.

In 2009, days before another fire, the sign that adorned the Moulin Rouge was moved to the Neon Boneyard museum, where it still awaits restoration.

Finally, in 2010, the Las Vegas City Council approved the razing of what was left of the Moulin Rouge.

In the 1950s,

the casino-resorts shifted away from intimate lounge acts to lavish spectaculars featuring "showgirls."

In 1957, *Minsky's Follies* at the Desert Inn introduced the first topless revue. The Sands Hotel had the Copa Girls, with extravagantly expensive productions.

The Stardust imported the *Lido de Paris* in 1958, and made that show its headline act.

In 1959, the Tropicana brought over the *Folies Bergere,* which had more than 29,000 performances there before it closed 50 years later.

*J*ubilee!

is the surviving descendant of the typical Vegas showgirl extravaganza, with a combination of lavish costumes, beautiful girls, and extraordinary special effects—like the sinking of the *Titanic* onstage.

In production at Bally's since 1981, *Jubilee!* also offers an "all-access backstage walking tour."

Showgirl dancers lead the tours, giving visitors a close-up look at the wild costumes, including the 20-pound headdresses, and firsthand insight into what it takes to put on a true spectacle.

The Sirens of Treasure Island

is an 18-minute extravaganza that includes singing, dancing, sword fights, pyrotechnics, and a shipwreck.

The pop opera is free, and it is performed four times a day in a tank containing a million gallons of "gray" water—wastewater reclaimed from the hotel.

The show's creator, Kenny Ortega, is best known as the choreographer of the original film *Dirty Dancing* and the director of *High School Musical*.

For the first quarter-century

of Las Vegas casino history, everything focused on bringing gamblers to the tables.

All the Hollywood stars—the singers, the dancers, the stage acts—were all loss-leaders meant to attract audiences that would spend money gambling.

That changed in 1969, when Elvis Presley agreed to perform at the newly built International for $125,000 a week.

In the first month, the show had earned more than $2 million.

Wayne Newton

has performed more than 30,000 shows in Las Vegas, earning him the honorary title of "Mr. Las Vegas."

Newton began in show business at the age of six and he was in junior high school when he first started performing on stage at the Fremont Hotel.

Today, Newton holds the record as the highest-paid nightclub performer in history.

For a brief period

during the early 1980s, Wayne Newton was co-owner of the Aladdin Hotel.

A month after he bought it, NBC News reported that Newton had ties to the Mob.

Denying the report, Newton sued NBC and won, clearing his name.

Wayne Newton remained an owner of the Aladdin for less than two years before deciding he had had enough.

The Aladdin became the Planet Hollywood Resort and Casino in 2007.

Barbra Streisand

broke the record for ticket sales to a single concert when she appeared at the MGM Grand Hotel in Las Vegas on New Year's Eve in 1999.

Billed as her last paid public appearance, the event sold more than 12,000 tickets and grossed nearly $15 million.

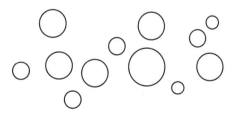

Where does a museum

commemorating the epic battle between organized crime and law enforcement belong if not Las Vegas?

The Mob Museum opened on February 14, 2012, the 83rd anniversary of the St. Valentine's Day Massacre in Chicago.

Located in the former federal courthouse, the museum is dedicated to preserving the story of how some of the most ruthless men in America contributed to the creation of the adult playground Las Vegas is today.

Howard Hughes,

the eccentric and reclusive billionaire, moved into the top two floors of the Desert Inn in 1966.

He was supposed to leave after 10 days, but he didn't want to. So he bought the place.

Then he bought the Sands, the Castaways, the Silver Slipper, and the Frontier.

One by one, Hughes cleaned out the gangsters who owned and operated Las Vegas by paying them off.

Hughes planned to buy the Stardust as well, but the Securities and Exchange Commission said no, fearing he would monopolize Las Vegas.

Today, Caesars Entertainment

owns the following casino-hotels in Las Vegas: Bally's, Caesars Palace, the Flamingo, Harrah's, the Imperial Palace, Paris Las Vegas, Planet Hollywood, Towers Westgate, and Rio.

MGM Resorts International owns the MGM Grand, Aria, Bellagio, Vdara, Mandalay Bay, the Mirage, Monte Carlo, New York-New York, Luxor, and Excalibur.

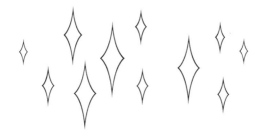

Originally, Nevada law

required background financial checks of *all* shareholders of *any* company that applied for a gaming license.

That meant it was virtually impossible for any company traded on a stock exchange to own a casino because it would have been too difficult to conduct a background check on every shareholder.

The 1967 Corporate Gaming Act changed that... *and* the future of Las Vegas.

Kirk Kerkorian bought the Flamingo hotel in 1968 and completed the International hotel the following year.

Then, he decided to build an even bigger place, the MGM Grand Hotel.

To raise money, Kerkorian sold the Flamingo and the International to the Hilton Corporation, and a new age had begun.

Before Hilton and Kerkorian,

the major source of funding for casino-resorts had been Mob money.

But even the Teamsters Union Pension Fund, which Jimmy Hoffa had made available to fund much of the growth in Las Vegas, was not enough to compete with the power of Wall Street.

And in the 1980s, when casino owner Steve Wynn and Wall Street financier Michael Milken figured out how to use junk bonds to raise the money they needed, it looked like there was no limit to what could be built.

Over the years,

there has been a dramatic change in the offerings of table games available in casinos on the Las Vegas Strip, based in large part on the tastes of gamblers.

In 1985, the big game was blackjack, accounting for 77 percent of the games and more than half of the casino table game revenue.

Today, blackjack accounts for barely half of the games and only a quarter of the revenue.

Craps has also decreased

its footprint on the Las Vegas Strip in the last 25 years, while roulette has increased slightly.

The big winner among the games during this shifting tide has been Baccarat, which now brings in more than 40 percent of the total casino table game revenue.

Games such as pai gow poker, that didn't even make it into the Strip statistics in 1985, are also increasing in popularity.

Las Vegas

is the lap of luxury, with more top-quality lodgings than any other city in the country, according to the AAA ratings.

A total of 10 hotels earned the Five-Diamond prize from the AAA travel editors, which is two more than second-place New York City.

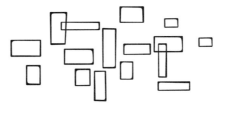

Bellagio

can claim an impressive 15 AAA Diamonds in all, which is pretty good for a rating system with five as the top prize.

In addition to the five diamonds it earned as a hotel, the Bellagio is also the home of two Five-Diamond restaurants: Le Cirque and Picasso.

Picasso could also qualify as a mini-gallery, with a number of the artist's masterpieces and ceramic works on display for diners.

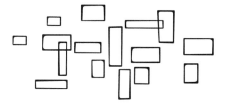

The Bellagio hotel

is a lot bigger than it looks, thanks to an optical illusion incorporated into its construction.

From a distance, what looks like a single window on the building's exterior is actually the portal into four rooms on two floors of the hotel.

Similar *trompes d'oeil* are used at Treasure Island and Caesars Palace.

The 50-story Wynn hotel

(and its sister building, the Encore) looks shorter from a distance because of the way it has been painted.

White stripes separate every *other* floor, making the building look like it only rises half the height.

Consider it an architectural reminder that not everything in Las Vegas is as it appears. (As if anyone needed reminding.)

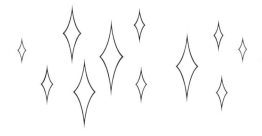

Aria at CityCenter

offers guests the kind of control they only *wish* they had at home.

The rooms themselves are programmed to welcome guests when they walk in: lights come on gradually; drapes open; a display of controls appears on the television screen.

Almost everything is controlled through the TV remote.

In addition to the *Jetsons* feel of it all, the automation provides both the guest and the hotel with the ability to manage settings to minimize energy use without compromising that sense of luxury people go to Las Vegas to experience in the first place.

CityCenter, the latest

addition to the Las Vegas skyline, was the largest privately funded construction project in U.S. history.

At a cost of $8.5 billion, MGM Resorts International built what might, in most other places, be considered a city of its own: 67 acres filled with a high-rise condominium, top-shelf hotels, a shopping mall, restaurants, public spaces, green parks, and art.

The place even generates electricity (with natural gas) and uses the "waste heat" to provide hot water throughout the complex.

Aria at CityCenter

is the largest building in the world to be Gold certified by the U.S. Green Building Council's LEED (Leadership in Energy and Environmental Design) program (one of *six* such honors for CityCenter).

Aria and the Vdara Hotel & Spa also earned Five-Key ratings from the Green Key Eco-Rating Program, which keeps track of the ecological sustainability of hotel operations.

A permanent fine arts

installation is incorporated into the public spaces of CityCenter, with sculptures by Maya Lin (who designed the Vietnam Veterans Memorial in Washington, D.C.) and by Henry Moore. A giant typewriter eraser by Claes Oldenburg and Coosje van Bruggen sits in Crystals Place, reminding people who recognize it that they are old enough to remember typewriter erasers.

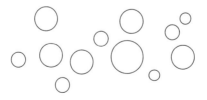

Even utopia can have its problems.

When it first opened, Vdara at the CityCenter was plagued by "solar convergence," when the shiny curves of the building focused the light and heat of the sun into what the local media called a "death ray."

MGM Resorts International also found itself locked in a legal dispute with builders over structural defects in the 26-story Harmon Hotel.

The builder says it can fix the building, given the chance.

MGM wants to implode the building, saying it isn't safe to leave standing.

At the turn of the 21st century,

when credit was cheap and building was easy, whenever Las Vegas was finished using a hotel, the building was imploded by demolition experts as onlookers thrilled to the sight of a building collapsing in on itself.

Notable implosions in Las Vegas history include:

2007: New Frontier and Stardust

2006: Boardwalk, Bourbon Street, and Castaways

2001: Desert Inn

2000: El Rancho

1998: Aladdin

1997: Hacienda

1996: Sands

1995: Landmark

1993: Dunes

Despite the lack of a casino,

the Mandarin Oriental at CityCenter won five AAA diamonds *and* five stars from Forbes Travel Guide.

Forbes also awarded five stars to the hotel's 27,000-square-foot luxury spa, which spans two floors and recalls the opulence of 1930s Shanghai.

In fact, the Mandarin Oriental enjoyed the coveted Forbes triple-crown victory in 2011, when its 23rd-floor signature restaurant, *Twist by Pierre Gagnaire, also* earned five stars.

Apparently, the decision to leave gambling off the table was a bet that paid off!

Two thousand colorful,

hand-blown glass blossoms suspended from the ceiling are among the first things visitors see on entering the Bellagio hotel. Made from approximately 3,000 individual glass pieces, "Fiori di Como" is a massive chandelier created by sculptor-artist Dale Chihuly.

The Bellagio Gallery of Fine Art houses exhibitions from museums around the world, and the Conservatory & Botanical Gardens provide a year-round home for rare plants and flowers.

No one need worry, however, that the Bellagio has lost sight of what is *really* important: It is also the home of the world's largest chocolate fountain.

The site of the old Dunes hotel

golf course became the Fountains of Bellagio in 1998. The 8.5-acre lake, with its 1,200+ geysers, cost $40 million to build.

More than 30 songs have been choreographed for the dancing water sprays to perform, sometimes spurting as high as 460 feet into the air.

A computer monitors weather conditions to determine whether the show can go on—occasionally cancelling or scaling down the performance, depending on the way the wind is blowing.

In 2008, the Mirage unveiled

Volcano 2.0, a fire-breathing display that erupts hourly, five times a night, to the delight of anyone standing in front of the hotel.

Flames and water spout from the top of a 30-foot-high man-made mountain, synchronized to a soundtrack composed by Grateful Dead drummer Mickey Hart and Zakir Hussain, famed percussionist from India.

From the surrounding lagoon, fireballs are launched 12 feet into the air using technology developed by the same company that built the Fountains of Bellagio.

Guests checking into the Mirage

will find themselves facing a 20,000-gallon saltwater aquarium stocked with more than a thousand coral reef animals from around the world.

The sharks, stingrays, eels, and other fish swim behind the front desk, on the other side of an acrylic wall that is 53-feet long and four-inches thick.

The fish are real, however the coral is not. Designers created an artificial coral environment designed to evoke what divers see in the Great Barrier Reef of Australia.

The Shark Reef Aquarium

at the Mandalay Bay Resort and Casino is the only predator-based aquarium and exhibit in North America.

It also provides the only scuba-diving opportunity in Las Vegas.

Certified divers are welcome to enter the tank and swim with more than 100 species of marine animals, including 15 varieties of shark.

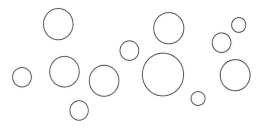

Non-diving visitors

to the Shark Reef Aquarium are also treated to a panoramic underwater view, as they walk through acrylic tunnels in the habitat.

In addition to entertaining and educating the public, the $60 million aquarium is home to a number of conservation and research initiatives.

It is also the only facility in Nevada accredited by the Association of Zoos and Aquariums.

It wouldn't be Las Vegas

without an aquarium that includes live mermaids putting on a show, but the Silverton Casino stepped up to make sure *that* particular civic need is met.

In the Mermaid Lounge (where else?), five young ladies with synchro-nized-swimming skills join 4,000 fish, some stingrays, and sharks inside an 117,000-gallon tank, to put on a real-live mermaid show, Thursday through Sunday.

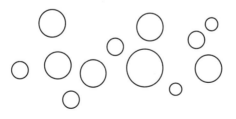

The Alliance

of Marine Parks and Aquariums has given its seal of approval to Siegfried & Roy's Dolphin Habitat at the Mirage.

The primary focus of the habitat (and the adjacent Secret Garden) is said to be scientific research and education, but even common visitors are welcome to become "trainers for a day."

The day-trainers get to spend time in the water with the dolphins and up to two "observers" are allowed to accompany each day-trainer for an extra charge.

Siegfried & Roy's

Secret Garden is home to several breeds of very big cats. A tropical environment has been constructed to mimic the natural habitat of the tigers, lions, panthers, and leopards that reside there.

The habitat also houses rare white lions and white tigers, which are a genetic variation (as opposed to being albinos).

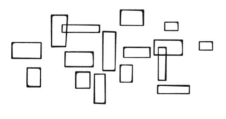

Looking for the *Titanic?*

It's in Las Vegas, of course.

Not all of it, perhaps, but the largest piece ever recovered can be found in *Titanic: The Artifact Exhibition* at the Luxor. That would be a 26-foot-long, 15-ton piece of the "unsinkable" ship's hull.

Smaller items on display include jewelry, dishes, documents, and gambling chips (it's Las Vegas, remember?).

In all, 300 artifacts and many more replicas make up the exhibit, as well as the stories of the passengers and an iceberg. Really.

Even a parking garage

in Las Vegas can be a spectacle.

On the fifth floor of the self-park facility at the Imperial Palace, 300 classic cars sit on display for anyone who cares to see them.

And not the same 300 every day! The collection rotates.

The Auto Collections provides a variety of cars to ogle, from Rolls-Royces to VW Bugs, from World War II Jeeps to rare Duesenbergs.

Old car commercials are shown, a seating area is available, and, of course, there is a gift shop.

Just another Las Vegas garage.

Beauty

isn't always only skin deep in Las Vegas.

Sometimes the real strength can only be seen under the hood.

That's certainly true at Shelby American, the company that has been making high-performance muscle cars since 1962.

Tours are available at Shelby's headquarters in Las Vegas, where some of the most famous cars ever produced—like the Cobra CSX2000 and the Terlingua—are on display.

The Las Vegas Motor Speedway

offers real racing, on a real racetrack, in real racecars, to wannabe racers.

The Exotics Racing school provides the instruction and the car, ranging from the "lowly" Porsche Cayman R to a Lamborghini with a V10 engine. (Knowledge of manual transmissions is not required.)

Once school is out, the student drivers are let loose on a five-lap tour of the track, after which they receive graduate certificates and are sent back to the freeway in their own cars.

Be very afraid.

Like almost anything else

in Las Vegas, auto racing can also be an indoor sport.

Fast Lap provides gasoline-powered go-karts with top-speeds of 50 mph and an opportunity to race other drivers around a 1,200-foot track.

Packages are available for people who want to combine car racing with firing a machine gun.

For a cleaner, quieter track,

Pole Position Raceway has invested in an all-electric go-kart fleet.

The driver is inches off the ground and powers along a course at speeds of up to 45 mph with as many as a dozen other drivers.

After each race, drivers are provided with SpeedSheet, a printed analysis of their performance.

Helmets and closed shoes are required. (The track provides the former, but not the latter.)

Walk Score ranks Las Vegas

as the 25th most walkable city in America, and nearly a third of visitors say they get around on foot.

Nevertheless, there are nearly a thousand taxis, more than 300 limousines, and at least 16 different bus companies in the city.

All that is in addition to the monorail!

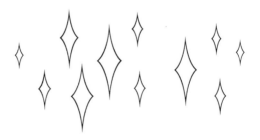

The Las Vegas Monorail

is the only privately owned public transportation company in the United States.

With seven stops along a 3.9-mile track, the fully automated system connects the various hotels and attractions along the Las Vegas Strip.

The track is only 26 inches wide, and it runs 30 feet off the ground.

The Monorail began operations in 2004 and carried its 50 millionth rider less than seven years later.

Plain water

is what brought people to Las Vegas in the first place, but that can be hard to remember when faced with the smorgasbord of activity on the Strip today.

At the Springs Preserve, the water has been gone since 1962, but the history is still in plain view, both along a series of hiking trails *and* indoor exhibits designed to educate visitors about the history and development of the land and its people.

The 180-acre site includes a restaurant operated by the Culinary Academy of Las Vegas and a 1,800-seat outdoor amphitheatre.

Once a year,

Springs Preserve hosts an all-you-can-eat Ice Cream Festival.

It's in May.

For all other days of the year, the smart money in town is on Luv-It Frozen Custard on Oakey Boulevard.

A family-run business opened in 1973, it has managed to draw customers almost entirely by word-of-mouth.

In 1950,

President Harry Truman authorized the
Nevada Test Site as a place for testing
nuclear weapons. With mushroom clouds
clearly visible from Las Vegas, only
65 miles away, the atomic bomb blasts
became a draw for tourists and created a
business boom for locals.

More than 900 nuclear tests were
conducted before the program was
ended in 1992.

Although atomic testing

no longer occurs around Las Vegas, the Atomic Testing Museum has worked hard to capture the afterglow.

In fact, the museum became Nevada's first and only official "national" museum, when the U.S. Congress designated it as the national depository for all items dealing with the country's nuclear testing programs.

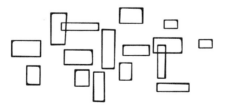

The world's largest

golden nugget is housed in (where else?) the lobby of the Golden Nugget hotel and casino.

Kevin Hillier found it with his metal detector back in the spring of 1980. The "Hand of Faith," as it is called, was buried outside his trailer in Australia, barely a foot below ground.

The Golden Nugget paid a million dollars for the 61-pound mascot, which is a little more than $1,100 per troy ounce.

Forget neon!

The brightest light in Vegas, if not the world, is pointed into space nightly from the top of the pyramid-shaped Luxor hotel.

Visible from 250 miles away, the narrow beam of light is generated by 39 xenon lamps and focused with computer-designed, curved mirrors.

According to the hotel, "an astronaut could read a newspaper by Luxor's Sky Beam from 10 miles into space."

*P*inball wizard alert:

A Pinball Hall of Fame has landed in Las Vegas.

More than 60 years of pinball history is represented, and it's all hands-on.

Hundreds of machines are waiting to be played.

The museum has no entrance fee. The only cost to patrons is what they feed into the coin slot, and the museum operators say those quarters wind up going to charities such as the Salvation Army.

Three people dead.

Fifteen suspects.

A matter of minutes to solve the crime?

Only on television... or at *CSI: The Experience.*

Visitors inspect the crime scene looking for clues, then move to a crime lab with interactive equipment.

Amateur crime scene investigators test their own theories as to what happened before witnessing a re-enactment of the event.

CSI diplomas are available for purchase at the gift shop.

Immediately following

the terrorist attacks of September 11, 2001, people in Las Vegas spontaneously began creating a tribute at the foot of the Statue of Liberty replica at the New York-New York Hotel and Casino.

Over the next few days, mourners left flowers, notes, T-shirts, and many other pieces of memorabilia, creating an impromptu shrine to those who lost their lives.

In response to the outpouring of emotion, the hotel management created a granite display case for a permanent *Tribute to Our Heroes* exhibition.

Paris was never like this.

Granted, the Eiffel Tower in the *other* Paris is twice as big, but the one at Paris Las Vegas provides a view of the mountains and desert, in addition to pyramids and the New York skyline.

The Louvre, the Opera House, the Hotel de Ville? Vegas has those covered, too. Just the façades, though, not the insides.

A two-thirds replica of the Arc de Triomphe stands outside the Paris Las Vegas, commemorating the names and dates of the Emperor Napoleon's conquests—just like that *other* one.

So there.

Las Vegas

offers many opportunities to tour the world without leaving town, including a tasting fleet of international sodas at the Coca-Cola Store.

For a few dollars, carbonation connoisseurs can get a tray full of plastic cups and find out what passes for refreshment in other parts of the world.

That, plus an elevator ride inside the world's largest Coke bottle (four stories tall), keeps the place pretty crowded.

RM Seafood

at the Mandalay Bay offers its own challenge: a blind tasting of 16 different ice creams. Get 'em all right, and the dish is free.

Be prepared, however, for some very challenging flavors offered up by chef Rick Moonen, like gazpacho or chocolate-chili... or combinations for which you must identify *all* the flavors for your guess to be deemed correct.

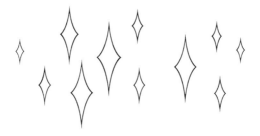

147

The entrance to the MGM Grand Hotel

is graced with a 45-foot-tall statute of a lion sitting on a 25-foot-tall pedestal.

The sculpture weighs a half-ton and is made of 1,660 pieces of bronze welded together.

Installed in 1997, the lion is said to be the largest bronze sculpture in the Western Hemisphere.

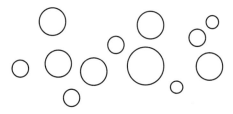

A 126-foot tall,

neon-lit clown marks the location of Circus Circus.

Lucky, as he is known, was recognized by *The Guinness Book of World Records* as the world's largest freestanding sign when he was first built in 1968.

When Lucky's 15,000 incandescent bulbs were replaced with fluorescent panels recently, the amount of electricity saved was enough to power nearly 200 average American homes.

The largest freestanding sign

in the world today is the one that identifies the Las Vegas Hotel (formerly the Las Vegas Hilton, and the International before that).

At 279 feet, the sign has a total area of more than 70,000 square feet and is lit with more than 6 miles of neon and fluorescent lights.

Jay Sarno,

who owned Caesars Palace at the time, opened Circus Circus in 1968 as a hybrid offering of big-top acts and casino gambling. This novel combination offered entertainment for the whole family, as trapeze artists performed over the gaming tables and juggling clowns walked among the customers.

Hotel rooms were added in 1972, and a new concept of Las Vegas entertainment began to take hold.

In case the circus

of Circus Circus isn't enough entertainment, the world's largest permanent big top is also home to America's largest indoor theme park, Adventuredome.

A variety of thrill rides provide plenty of g-forces, speed, and spin, while more traditional fare—like a Ferris wheel and a merry-go-round—are available, too.

Adventuredome opened in 1993, at a cost of $90 million. It is 200 feet high and enclosed by nearly 9,000 panes of glass that weigh more than 300 pounds each.

Chuck Jones

was an advocate for creativity, and the Oscar-winning artist practiced what he preached.

Bugs Bunny, Daffy Duck, the Road Runner, and a host of other iconic figures were all products of his 60-year career as an animator and filmmaker.

Today his work to inspire imagination in others continues in the Chuck Jones Experience.

In addition to original artwork, the Experience includes interactive exhibits, film clips, and interviews with Jones himself.

Visitors can try their hands at drawing animations or generating sound effects for some of their favorite cartoons.

Where does Hollywood go

to test its television shows? Las Vegas, of course.

The CBS Television Research Center in the MGM Grand screens pilots for shows from CBS, MTV, Nickelodeon, and other Viacom networks.

Visitors watch the program using test pads and monitors to communicate their reactions, then they take a short survey about what they saw.

Commercials, websites, and tech-toys also get rated by the public at the Center, which is free and open daily.

Art in Las Vegas

has its own emergency room: the former Fremont Medical Arts building.

The idea behind Emergency Arts is to bring together creative talent from all fields to form a cooperative collective.

From galleries to design firms, yoga studios to start-up nonprofits, a wide range of professional artists began gravitating to the downtown area in early 2012.

With a coffee shop and a common-space gallery, Emergency Arts is meant as a place where the public is part of the effort to keep art in Las Vegas alive.

Emergency Arts

is one of the venues that celebrates First Friday, a monthly event to bring attention to the young artists of Las Vegas.

On the first Friday of every month, from 6 p.m. to midnight, the streets in the Downtown Arts District are filled with artists, vendors, food, and music.

Most of the galleries are also open, and some even offer a "Preview Thursday" for those who are crowd-averse.

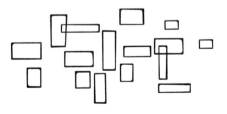

When Hoover Dam

was nearing completion, in 1935, Las Vegas officials worried that once the workers had departed it would be tough to replace them as a revenue source.

Enter Clyde Zerby, an experienced showman who knew how to throw a town-wide party. He suggested a festival to attract tourism.

The local Elks lodge liked the idea, and Helldorado Days were born.

The modern Helldorado Days,

the longest-running civic event in Las Vegas, still evoke a sense of the Old West.

Visitors can enjoy a four-day rodeo, a parade, trail rides, poker tournaments, and a general carnival atmosphere.

Many of the local men stop shaving on a specified date so they can participate in the Whiskerino beard-growing competition.

The first Helldorado, in 1935,

was held in a tent village near Sixth and Fremont. The theme was the Wild West, and visitors came to have their pictures taken with local business people wearing rented Hollywood movie costumes.

Helldorado became an annual event that grew bigger every year.

In 1946, footage from the parade was even included in the Roy Rogers' film, *Heldorado*.

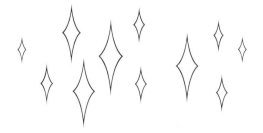

By 1948,

Helldorado had grown so big, it needed more space.

Local businessman "Big Jim" Cashman spearheaded the effort to build a stadium large enough to house a rodeo.

Once it was built, the stadium also attracted a minor league baseball team, the Las Vegas Wranglers.

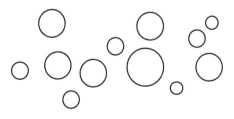

Today, Cashman Field Center

is a $26-million complex that sprawls over 50 acres. It includes a 9,334-seat stadium and a 100,000-square-foot convention center.

Built in 1983 on land donated by the Cashman family, the entire facility is owned by the Las Vegas Convention and Visitors Authority.

Cashman Field is the home of the Las Vegas 51s, a minor league franchise named after the nearby legendary Area 51.

Cashman Field

is the home of Big League Weekend, when Major League Baseball sends teams to entertain the fans of Las Vegas.

The event is part of MLB spring training, and it serves a variety of purposes:

- The city sees it as a publicity opportunity to attract future visitors from around the country who watch the games on television.
- The fans in Las Vegas love the opportunity to see big leaguers play ball.
- Wishful thinkers hope it will lead to the day when Las Vegas will be able to host its own Major League Baseball team.

Baseball fans

who spend the summer touring the country hoping to see every major league ballpark are wasting their time.

Big League Dreams makes it possible to visit six of them without ever leaving Las Vegas.

Granted, the replica fields are scaled down versions and only softball is really played on any of them.

But it's a good way to satisfy the curiosity of anyone who longs for a look at Fenway Park, Wrigley Field, Yankee Stadium, Dodger Stadium, Angel Stadium, and Crosley Field all in the same day.

Leave it to Las Vegas

to break up a couple like Oklahoma and professional rodeo.

The Sooner State had hosted the Wrangler National Finals Rodeo (NFR) for 20 years when, in 1984, Las Vegas guaranteed a prize fund of more than double what Oklahoma had offered.

The Wrangler NFR has been held in Las Vegas ever since.

The World Series of Poker

is held each year at the Rio All-Suite Hotel and Casino in Las Vegas.

Players from more than 100 nations play for a share of hundreds of millions of dollars in prize money.

Anyone who is over 21 years old and can afford the buy-in can play.

Satellite tournaments are cheaper to enter (as low as $500), and the winner of each round moves up to take a seat at the next level.

A seat at the final round can cost $1 million.

The tournament runs from May to July.

The SoBe Ice Arena

in Las Vegas has a full-size, NHL-regulation indoor ice rink. When it's not being used by hockey leagues in different age ranges, the rink is available for public skating.

Equipment is available for rental. And a casino is located in the same complex!

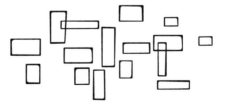

Like all manners of entertainment

in Las Vegas, bowling is serious business.

In fact, the first athletic organization founded at the University of Nevada, Las Vegas, was a bowling team.

Actually, it was 1957, so there was no UNLV, really. It was called Nevada Southern. But it *did* have a bowling team that met Thursday nights!

167

More than half-a-dozen

bowling alleys in town offer more than 60 lanes each, and several are open 24 hours a day.

In 2012 bowling tournaments in Las Vegas included...

- the Pan American Bowling Confederation Combined Championships,
- the Burlesque Hall of Fame's Barecats Invitational 2012 Bowl-Off,
- the 14th Annual Punk Rock Bowling & Music Festival,
- the 29th Annual Las Vegas Showgirl Invitational Bowling Tournament,
- the 55th Annual Military Bowling Championships, and
- the 2nd Annual Kailiha'o Hula Bowling Tournament.

For people who like

their bowling a little more private, the Palms Casino Resort offers the Kingpin Suite.

The suite measures more than 4,000 square feet and includes two full-size, regulation bowling lanes. With two bedrooms and three bathrooms, a wet bar, and a pool table, there is plenty of room for 100 people to bowl the night away.

Basketball aficionados

can gather 350 people into the Palms Casino Resort Hardwood Suite, which the hotel says "replicates the lifestyle of a NBA superstar."

These hotel accommodations cover 10,000 square feet on two floors, and include a basketball half-court, professional locker room, dance floor, and Jacuzzi tub.

(The list of amenities also includes hair dryer and ironing board, but that has to be a joke, right?)

For the sports-challenged,

the Palms has a collection of other fantasy
suites, including:

- Hugh Hefner Sky Villa (with an
  "extra-large show tub"),
- Barbie Suite (with that Malibu Dream
  House feel),
- Crib Suite (hip-hop style with a DJ
  booth and hydraulic bed),
- Erotic Suite (leather, metal, mirrored
  ceilings, and a round rotating bed).

Las Vegas

is the unofficial Ninth Hawaiian Island. According to the 2010 U.S. Census, the number of "non-Hispanic Pacific Islanders" living in Clark County had more than doubled in a decade—to more than 12,000.

Many transplanted Hawaiians say they don't worry about missing friends and family, because at the rate fellow islanders come to Las Vegas to vacation and gamble, sooner or later, they'll all see each other again!

The "Aloha Spirit"

is alive and well in Las Vegas, and it is celebrated at least once a year with the Annual Pure Aloha Spring Festival & Concerts.

The four-day event is held in April, providing plenty of cultural performances, food, and music.

And for people who miss it, there's always Lei Day, also celebrated annually, in May.

Viva Las Vegas.

Not just an Elvis movie.

It's a Rockabilly party, celebrating all things nostalgic (which is defined by the promoters as pre-1963).

In addition to music and dancing, the four-day event in April includes a vintage fashion show, a tiki pool party, a classic car display, and a burlesque competition.

The 15th annual Viva Las Vegas was held at the Orleans Hotel and added bowling and burlesque-bingo to the roster of activities.

Music lovers

have plenty to celebrate in Las Vegas.

The annual City of Lights Jazz & R&B Festival marked its twentieth year in the spring of 2012.

Caribbean culture, food, and rhythm are highlighted at the Reggae in the Desert festival in June.

For more than a decade, the International Mariachi Festival has taken place at the Paris Las Vegas Hotel.

The Extreme Thing Sports & Music Festival

serves as the start to the BMX dirt bike riding season.

Bikers ride down a 40-foot drop into 12 feet of dirt, followed by a jump over a 25-foot gap, to entertain the fans *and* to qualify for invitational events that occur later in the year.

Add that to the amateur skateboarding competition, the mixed martial arts demonstration, and the cage match between the professional wrestlers of Adrenaline Unleashed, and it's easy to see how Extreme Thing earned its name.

Cannes? Sundance? Holly-who?

Las Vegas is home to more film festivals than any cine-maven (who also has to make a living) could ever hope to attend.

Here's just a sample:

- Las Vegas Film Festival
- Las Vegas Jewish Film Festival
- Las Vegas Comedy Film Fest
- PollyGrind Underground Film Festival
- Vegas Independent Film Festival
- International Vegas Cine Fest
- Nevada Film Festival
- Las Vegas Latino Short Film Festival
- Las Vegas Student Film Festival
- UNLV Spring Flicks

At KISS—by Monster Mini Golf,

there are the obligatory 18 holes of miniature golf, festooned with black lights, lasers, and an array of kitsch reminders of the legendary rock band.

But the "Hotter Than Hell" wedding chapel takes this Las Vegas attraction to a whole new level:

- Invitations printed as concert tickets,
- The ceremony on a stage with theatrical lights, sound, and a fog machine,
- KISS costumes to wear,
- Guitar picks to throw like rice,
- Even a real guitar to smash—to be framed and presented later as a souvenir of the blessed event.

Flash floods

can occur in Las Vegas at any time, and they can be deadly.

Rapidly moving water just 6 inches deep is enough to knock a person down and cause drowning.

To combat this natural threat, the city has built hundreds of miles of underground tunnels to channel the water, and hundreds more are on the drawing board.

Oblivious to the danger, nearly 700 people are said to have built makeshift homes in those tunnels.

Las Vegas

is the suicide capital of the United States.

The average is about one suicide a day.

Residents of Las Vegas have a 50 percent higher risk of dying by their own hands than residents of other cities.

Visitors to Las Vegas run an even higher risk of suicide than residents.

Aviation arrived in Las Vegas

in 1920, when Randall Henderson and Jake Beckley landed an old Curtiss "Jenny" biplane in Harry Anderson's field on May 17.

By November, Anderson Field had been transformed into an airworthy landing strip and was opened as Las Vegas's first airport on Thanksgiving Day.

Anderson Field (later renamed Rockwell Field) was located near the intersection of today's Sahara and Paradise Avenues.

In the 1920s Las Vegas

served as a way station for the nascent aviation industry much the same as it had been for the railroads and for the intrepid pioneers crossing the desert on foot.

Pilots carrying passengers and mail across the country stopped in Las Vegas on their way to and from Los Angeles.

Western Air Express was the first airline to service the route, and Maury Graham piloted the first airmail flight out of Las Vegas on April 17, 1926.

Passenger traffic

didn't begin to fly in and out of Las Vegas until a month after the U.S. Mail did.

In May 1926 two guys paid to wear coveralls and sit on mailbags at the front of a Douglas M-2 biplane.

Two weeks later, Maude Campbell became the first woman to arrive by air.

She paid $160 for a round-trip ticket from Salt Lake City to Los Angeles that included a stop in Las Vegas.

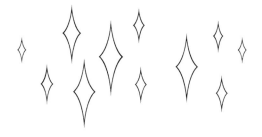

Two Las Vegas airports

have been named after Senator Pat McCarran, who authored the 1929 Civil Aeronautics Act.

Western Airfield, named for the airline, was renamed McCarran Airport in 1941.

When the United States entered World War II, the Army Air Corps needed a training facility.

Las Vegas was ideal: relative safety from enemy attack, year-round flying conditions, and uninhabited land to use for target practice.

The U.S. Army Air Corps Gunnery School opened at McCarran Airport in 1942 and operated until the end of the war.

In 1947 the military

returned and reestablished its base at McCarran Airport.

It was eventually renamed for Lieutenant William H. Nellis, a former Las Vegas High School student who lost his life as a fighter pilot during World War II.

Today, Nellis Air Force Base is the home of the supersonic military aerobatic team, the Thunderbirds.

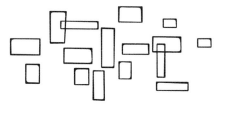

In 1948, after the Air Force

returned to Las Vegas and reclaimed
McCarran Airport, civil aviation had
to find a new home.

The private owner of Alamo Field
sold it to Clark County to be used as the
new airport, which was rededicated as
McCarran Field.

Four airlines—Bonanza, Western,
Transcontinental Western (TWA), and
United—served McCarran Field when it
opened.

Las Vegas-based

Bonanza Air Lines called itself the nation's first all-jet powered commercial carrier.

In 1958 Bonanza started buying turbo-jet aircraft.

In 1960 with the retirement of its last propeller powered DC-3, Bonanza ushered in the all-jet age.

Bonanza ultimately merged into a company that was bought by Howard Hughes to become Hughes Air West, which was bought by Republic Airlines, which was bought by Northwest, which merged with Delta... which is still around.

In 2010 Las Vegas's

McCarran International Airport ranked as the eighth busiest in North America.

In 2011 more than 41 million passengers flew in and out on commercial flights.

Photographs and artifacts from the early days of aviation in Las Vegas are on display 24 hours a day at the Howard W. Cannon Aviation Museum located in Terminal 2 (and various other locations) at McCarran International Airport.

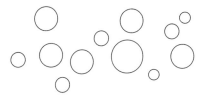

Howard W. Cannon

was the U.S. Senator from Nevada who sponsored the airline deregulation act of 1978.

While many communities lost service when the federal government decided to allow airlines to fly wherever they wanted to, that's not what happened in Las Vegas.

Number of airlines flying to McCarran International *before* deregulation: 5.

Number of airlines servicing the airport five years later: 17.

That's why the aviation museum was named after Cannon in 1999.

While passengers

at other airports around the country must lug their baggage to the airport before they can check it in, air travelers in Las Vegas have another option.

Bags-to-Go has set up an exclusive deal with a number of airlines so passengers can check in their bags at their hotels.

Then they can spend one more day on the town before heading to the airport for their flight home.

In 1957 the Hacienda Hotel and Casino

entered the airline business, after a fashion.

To entice gamblers from Los Angeles, the Hacienda offered a package for $27.50 that included round-trip airfare, a night in a deluxe room, a bottle of champagne, $5 in casino chips, and a tote bag.

By 1961 the Hacienda fleet of aircraft were bringing more people into the airport than all the commercial airlines combined.

Such junket flights, as they were called, were brought to an end by the federal government in 1962.

The military effort

in World War II generated a substantial income for the residents of Las Vegas because of the U.S. Army Air Corps Gunnery School and local magnesium production.

Later, in peacetime, the business community turned to tourism as a replacement industry.

The Las Vegas Chamber of Commerce launched the Livewire Fund, raising $84,000 in 1945 (and more in later years) to get the word out about the joys of their desert town.

A careful combination of advertising and publicity helped to increase the number of tourists to 8 million by 1953.

Getting high in Las Vegas

has never been easier.

Okay, it's never really been that hard, but the Stratosphere Tower is this country's tallest freestanding observation tower (1,149 feet), and it has an elevator.

If altitude alone isn't enough of an enticement, tourists who make it to the top have a choice of four thrill-rides to get the adrenaline pumping.

The latest addition includes the opportunity to jump from the 108th floor for a "controlled free-fall" experience sure to leave you breathless... and more than $100 poorer.

Some of the most interesting

things about the Stratosphere are the ones that *didn't* happen.

Originally, the owners wanted to make it 1,800 feet tall, but the Federal Aviation Administration said no.

A $6-million mechanical gorilla, à la King Kong, was proposed as a ride that would hold 48 people as it scaled the outside of the tower.

A roller coaster that would have screamed down the side of the tower at 120 mph and wound up on the other side of Las Vegas Boulevard also never got off the ground.

Sandra Kay Vaccaro

of Las Vegas is the only woman ever to be listed in the Nevada Black Book.

Well, it's not black, actually, and it's not really a book.

Officially called the "List of Excluded Persons," the Black Book enumerates all the people who are forbidden from setting foot in any of the state's casinos.

Vaccaro and her husband were convicted of an elaborate slot-cheating conspiracy.

Today, the University of Nevada, Las Vegas (UNLV)

is a respectable institution with a powerhouse basketball team.

In 1951, however, it was merely an extension program of the University of Nevada, Reno (UNR).

The first 28 students met in dressing rooms in the Las Vegas High School auditorium.

Six years later, Las Vegas had its own campus, by which time the students were known as the Rebels for their determination to break free of UNR.

UNLV was finally born in 1969, and within a decade it had surpassed its northern rival in total enrollment.

In 1973

UNLV Regent Helen Thomas came to a startling realization about the school for which she shared ultimate responsibility: the campus was too flat.

Not afraid to jump in where needed, Thomas donated $9,000 to remedy the situation, with the construction of a three-foot hill.

Evidence of the hill may be seen today embedded in the back of the alumni auditorium.

Las Vegas has segregated swimming pools,

each appealing to a different age group and pocketbook.

Many hotels offer adult pool parties, so the fun never has to stop.

And, since it's Vegas, there's the issue of nudity, or what the guidebooks now refer to as "European-style sunbathing."

It's available to everyone of a certain age, without regard to whether they really should be wearing clothes.

How about a day at the beach?

Yes, it's possible in Las Vegas.

The Mandalay Bay Beach is an 11-acre water park with a wave pool, a flowing river, and 2,700 tons of "real sand."

Cabanas, day beds, bungalows, and villas are all available, as well as three different swimming pools, none of which is far from food, drink, or, of course, gambling opportunities.

About the Author

Victor Dorff is a New Yorker living in Southern California and writing about the travel destinations that make the world such an interesting place to visit. His work has been seen on television, on the web, and on bookshelves around the country. He can be seen in airports, hotels, museums, restaurants, or anywhere there is a good story being told.